Letts

KS1 Success

Age 5-7

Times tables

Practice workbook

Simon Greaves and Angela Smith

About this book

Times tables

Times tables are an essential component of mathematics as they provide the building blocks for moving on to multiplication and division.

This book is designed to develop your child's times tables skills so that they can tackle them confidently and consistently at Key Stage 1.

Work through the book with your child and encourage them to revisit their favourite activities or repeat the activities for a particular times table that may be posing problems. It is a good idea to reward your child with praise, encouragement and little treats for mastering all or part of a times table.

Features of the book

- *Learn your tables* – introduce the times tables and help understanding.

- *Parent's notes* – provide ideas for motivating your child and suggest extra activities to do in everyday life.

- *Tables practice and activities* – a variety of tasks and questions to engage your child.

- *Test your tables* – short tests to see how well your child knows the times table.

- *Speed tests and progress charts* – timed challenges to help your child master times tables. The progress charts enable both you and your child to monitor progress on a regular basis.

- *Answers* to all the questions are in a pull-out booklet at the centre of the book.

ACKNOWLEDGEMENTS

The author and publisher are grateful to the copyright holders for permission to use quoted materials and images.

P04 © Tribalium; P05 © Mi.Ti.s; P06 © Tribalium; P12 © Tribalium; P18 © Tribalium; P24 © Tribalium; P30 © Tribalium; P44 © Thomas Amby; P48 © lineartestpilot, © Tribalium; P50 © notkoo; P56 © elmm; P58 © elmm

The above images have been used under license from Shutterstock.com

All other images are ©Jupiterimages or © Letts Educational, an imprint of HarperCollins Publishers Ltd

Every effort has been made to trace copyright holders and obtain their permission for the use of copyright material. The author and publisher will gladly receive information enabling them to rectify any error or omission in subsequent editions. All facts are correct at time of going to press.

Published by Letts Educational

An imprint of HarperCollins Publishers Ltd
1 London Bridge Street
London SE1 9GF

ISBN 9781844198702

First published 2013

This edition published 2015

10 9 8 7 6 5 4 3 2 1

Text and Design ©Letts Educational, an imprint of HarperCollins Publishers Ltd

British Library Cataloguing in Publication Data. A CIP record of this book is available from the British Library.

Commissioning Editor: Tammy Poggo

Authors: Simon Greaves and Angela Smith

Project Manager: Michelle I'Anson

Cover Design: Sarah Duxbury

Inside Concept Design: Ian Wrigley

Text, Design and Layout: Jouve India Private Limited

Printed and bound by RR Donnelley APS

Contents

Learn your tables

In the first times table the numbers from one to twelve are each multiplied by one. Multiplying a number by one gives an answer which is the same as the number itself.

1	×	1	=	1
2	×	1	=	2
3	×	1	=	3
4	×	1	=	4
5	×	1	=	5
6	×	1	=	6
7	×	1	=	7
8	×	1	=	8
9	×	1	=	9
10	×	1	=	10
11	×	1	=	11
12	×	1	=	12

Parent's note

Reward your child with a daily treat for learning all or part of a times table.

Encourage your child to use their fingers and thumbs to show the answers whilst reciting the one times table.

Tables practice

1. Write in the missing answer to complete each multiplication fact.

    $5 \times 1 = \boxed{}$ $12 \times 1 = \boxed{}$ $3 \times 1 = \boxed{}$

    $7 \times 1 = \boxed{}$ $4 \times 1 = \boxed{}$ $8 \times 1 = \boxed{}$

    $1 \times 1 = \boxed{}$ $11 \times 1 = \boxed{}$ $2 \times 1 = \boxed{}$

    $9 \times 1 = \boxed{}$ $10 \times 1 = \boxed{}$ $6 \times 1 = \boxed{}$

2. Write in the missing number to complete each multiplication fact.

    $\boxed{} \times 1 = 4$ $\boxed{} \times 1 = 6$ $\boxed{} \times 1 = 11$

    $\boxed{} \times 1 = 2$ $\boxed{} \times 1 = 7$ $\boxed{} \times 1 = 1$

    $\boxed{} \times 1 = 5$ $\boxed{} \times 1 = 3$ $\boxed{} \times 1 = 8$

    $\boxed{} \times 1 = 10$ $\boxed{} \times 1 = 12$ $\boxed{} \times 1 = 9$

Activities

1. Draw a line to join each multiplication to its answer.

    (2×1)   (4×1)   (6×1)   (9×1)   (3×1)

    9   3   2   6   4

2. A cabbage costs £1.

    Write down how many cabbages you can buy with:

    £2 $\boxed{}$ cabbages   £5 $\boxed{}$ cabbages

    £10 $\boxed{}$ cabbages   £12 $\boxed{}$ cabbages

    £3 $\boxed{}$ cabbages   £6 $\boxed{}$ cabbages

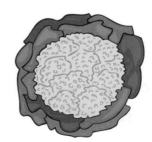

Two times table

Learn your tables

Multiplying by two is the same as doubling.

All the answers are even numbers.

An even number is one that ends with 0, 2, 4, 6 or 8.

1	×	2	=	2
2	×	2	=	4
3	×	2	=	6
4	×	2	=	8
5	×	2	=	10
6	×	2	=	12
7	×	2	=	14
8	×	2	=	16
9	×	2	=	18
10	×	2	=	20
11	×	2	=	22
12	×	2	=	24

Parent's note

A useful way to help your child learn a times table is to make up a rhyme. Here's an example for the two times table:

"2 fishes in a stream, 4 cats licking cream
6 budgies in a cage, 8 bulls in a rage…"

Tables practice

1. Write in the missing answer to complete each multiplication fact.

12 × 2 = ☐   5 × 2 = ☐   3 × 2 = ☐

1 × 2 = ☐   10 × 2 = ☐   11 × 2 = ☐

9 × 2 = ☐   2 × 2 = ☐   6 × 2 = ☐

7 × 2 = ☐   4 × 2 = ☐   8 × 2 = ☐

2. Write in the missing number to complete each multiplication fact.

☐ × 2 = 14   ☐ × 2 = 6   ☐ × 2 = 8

☐ × 2 = 2   ☐ × 2 = 12   ☐ × 2 = 22

☐ × 2 = 10   ☐ × 2 = 4   ☐ × 2 = 18

☐ × 2 = 20   ☐ × 2 = 16   ☐ × 2 = 24

Activities

1. Socks come in pairs. There are two socks in a pair. For each picture complete the tables fact to show how many socks there are in total.

4 × 2 = ☐

3 × 2 = ☐

☐ × 2 = ☐

☐ × 2 = ☐

2. Count the tokens in each box. Each token is worth 2. Write a multiplication to show how much each box of tokens is worth.

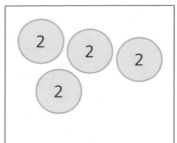 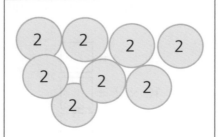 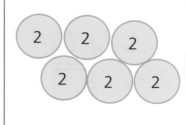

☐ × 2 = ☐   ☐ × 2 = ☐   ☐ × 2 = ☐

3. Draw a line to join each balloon to the correct present.

 7 × 2   2 × 2   8 × 2   3 × 2   9 × 2   11 × 2

 16    6    14    4    22    18

4. Circle the multiplication that matches the number in the box.

18	5 × 2	8 × 2	10 × 2	9 × 2
8	6 × 2	4 × 2	2 × 2	3 × 2
12	5 × 2	7 × 2	6 × 2	8 × 2
24	12 × 2	10 × 2	9 × 2	8 × 2

5. Colour in all the shapes that contain an answer in the two times table.

What can you see? _____

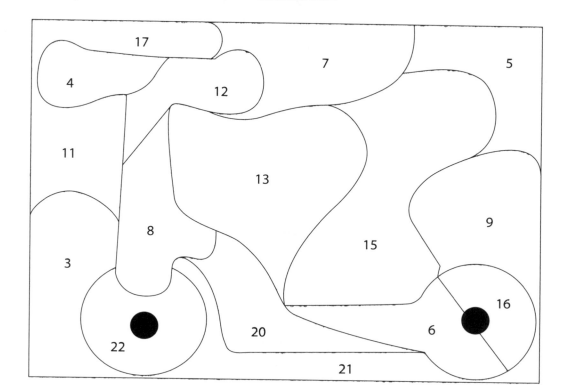

6. Here are some multiplications. Each one has the wrong answer.
Write the correct answer in the box.

5 × 2 = 12   ✗ ☐   3 × 2 = 16   ✗ ☐

9 × 2 = 14   ✗ ☐   12 × 2 = 22   ✗ ☐

7. Shade a path through the number grid. Only shade answers that are in the two times table.

13	21	23	16	10	→ End
5	3	7	24	29
7	11	1	22	33
15	18	4	8	39
2	6	19	25	29
12	9	17	27	31

Start →

8. Complete the multiplication table.

× 2	3	8	9	4	6	2	11
				8			

9. Work out the answer to each multiplication fact in the robot.

Use the colour code to colour the picture.

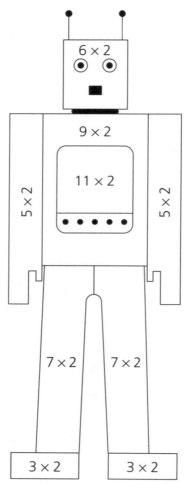

Colour code	
6	Red
10	Black
12	Purple
14	Blue
18	Grey
22	Yellow

10. Look at the numbers in the box. Circle the numbers that are answers in the two times table.

20   6   19

22   11   4

18   17   9   12

Test your tables

1. Write out the two times table.

1 × 2 = ☐

2 × 2 = ☐

☐ × ☐ = ☐

☐ × ☐ = ☐

☐ × ☐ = ☐

☐ × ☐ = ☐

☐ × ☐ = ☐

☐ × ☐ = ☐

☐ × ☐ = ☐

☐ × ☐ = ☐

☐ × ☐ = ☐

☐ × ☐ = ☐

2. Complete these multiplication facts.

☐ × 2 = 12

12 × 2 = ☐

☐ × 2 = 18

4 × 2 = ☐

☐ × 2 = 2

☐ × 2 = 16

7 × 2 = ☐

2 × 2 = ☐

11 × 2 = ☐

☐ × 2 = 6

5 × 2 = ☐

☐ × 2 = 20

Score   /12

Score   /12

Ten times table

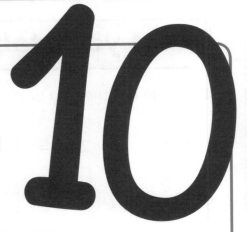

Learn your tables

All the answers in the ten times table end in 0.

All you need to do is write a zero after each of the numbers 1, 2, 3, 4, ... to get the answers. That's easy!

1	×	10	=	10
2	×	10	=	20
3	×	10	=	30
4	×	10	=	40
5	×	10	=	50
6	×	10	=	60
7	×	10	=	70
8	×	10	=	80
9	×	10	=	90
10	×	10	=	100
11	×	10	=	110
12	×	10	=	120

Parent's note

Call out an answer from the ten times table and ask your child to give you the tables fact to match the answer. This is a fun activity which can be done on a car journey or during a meal.

Encourage your child to use a skipping rope to skip whilst reciting the ten times table.

100

Tables practice

1. Write in the missing answer to complete each multiplication fact.

4 × 10 = 40

7 × 10 = 70

1 × 10 = 10

5 × 10 = 50

12 × 10 = ~~12~~ 120

3 × 10 = 30

9 × 10 = 90

11 × 10 = 110

2 × 10 = 20

8 × 10 = 80

10 × 10 = 100

6 × 10 = ☐

2. Write in the missing number to complete each multiplication fact.

☐ × 10 = 50

☐ × 10 = 80

☐ × 10 = 10

☐ × 10 = 30

☐ × 10 = 120

☐ × 10 = 70

☐ × 10 = 100

☐ × 10 = 20

☐ × 10 = 110

☐ × 10 = 90

☐ × 10 = 60

☐ × 10 = 40

Activities

1. The tree holds the answers to the ten times table. Find the answers on each part of the tree and complete the multiplication.

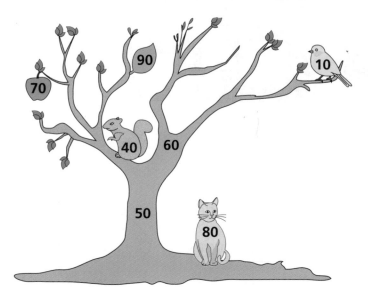

Cat ☐ × 10 = ☐

Branch ☐ × 10 = ☐

Apple ☐ × 10 = ☐

Squirrel ☐ × 10 = ☐

Bird ☐ × 10 = ☐

Trunk ☐ × 10 = ☐

Leaf ☐ × 10 = ☐

2. Count the tokens in each box. Each token is worth 10. Write a multiplication to show how much each box of tokens is worth.

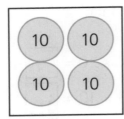

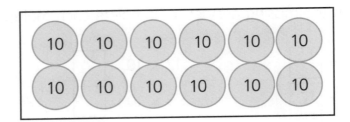

4 × 10 = ☐   ☐ × 10 = ☐

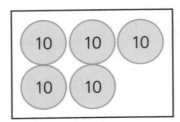

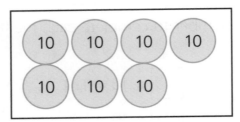

☐ × ☐ = ☐   ☐ × ☐ = ☐

3. This is a number machine. It multiplies numbers by ten. Write in the missing numbers.

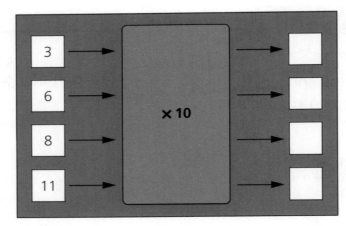

4. An orange costs 10p.

Write down how many oranges you can buy with:

20p ☐ oranges   50p ☐ oranges

40p ☐ oranges   80p ☐ oranges

30p ☐ oranges   £1.20 ☐ oranges

5. Draw a line from each rocket to the planet with the correct answer.

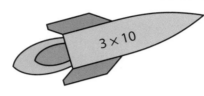

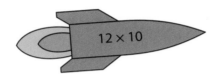

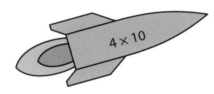

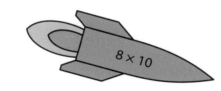

6. Here are some multiplications. Each one has the wrong answer.
Write the correct answer in the box.

3 × 10 = 50   ✗ ☐   1 × 10 = 20   ✗ ☐

2 × 10 = 60   ✗ ☐   7 × 10 = 110   ✗ ☐

12 × 10 = 100   ✗ ☐   5 × 10 = 70   ✗ ☐

7. Fill in the missing numbers by counting on or back in tens.

20	☐	40	☐	☐	☐	☐
50	60	☐	☐	☐	☐	☐
80	70	☐	☐	☐	☐	20
120	☐	100	☐	☐	☐	☐

Ten times table

8. Draw a line to join each multiplication to its answer.

(3 × 10)   (5 × 10)   (6 × 10)   (11 × 10)   (9 × 10)

| 50 | | 110 | | 30 | | 90 | | 60 |

9. Complete these tables facts.

5 × 10 = ☐

8 × ☐ = 80

☐ × 10 = 110

☐ × 10 = 20

4 × 10 = ☐

☐ × 10 = 100

9 × 10 = ☐

1 × 10 = ☐

10. Circle the multiplication that matches the number in the box.

100	10 × 10	11 × 10	12 × 10	9 × 10
80	3 × 10	8 × 10	6 × 10	7 × 10
70	7 × 10	1 × 10	8 × 10	10 × 10
90	11 × 10	9 × 10	8 × 10	6 × 10

Test your tables

1. Write out the ten times table.

$1 \times 10 = \boxed{}$

$2 \times 10 = \boxed{}$

$\boxed{} \times \boxed{} = \boxed{}$

$\boxed{} \times \boxed{} = \boxed{}$

$\boxed{} \times \boxed{} = \boxed{}$

$\boxed{} \times \boxed{} = \boxed{}$

$\boxed{} \times \boxed{} = \boxed{}$

$\boxed{} \times \boxed{} = \boxed{}$

$\boxed{} \times \boxed{} = \boxed{}$

$\boxed{} \times \boxed{} = \boxed{}$

$\boxed{} \times \boxed{} = \boxed{}$

$\boxed{} \times \boxed{} = \boxed{}$

2. Complete these multiplication facts.

$4 \times 10 = \boxed{}$

$\boxed{} \times 10 = 70$

$1 \times 10 = \boxed{}$

$\boxed{} \times 10 = 120$

$\boxed{} \times 10 = 50$

$\boxed{} \times 10 = 60$

$8 \times 10 = \boxed{}$

$2 \times 10 = \boxed{}$

$10 \times 10 = \boxed{}$

$\boxed{} \times 10 = 30$

$\boxed{} \times 10 = 110$

$9 \times 10 = \boxed{}$

Score /12

Score /12

Five times table

Learn your tables

You can work out the answers to the five times table by halving the answers in the ten times table.

All the answers in the five times table end in 5 or 0.

1	×	5	=	5
2	×	5	=	10
3	×	5	=	15
4	×	5	=	20
5	×	5	=	25
6	×	5	=	30
7	×	5	=	35
8	×	5	=	40
9	×	5	=	45
10	×	5	=	50
11	×	5	=	55
12	×	5	=	60

Parent's note

Use piles of 5p coins to make different multiplication facts, for example, five 5p coins to show 5 × 5 = 25.

Throw a tennis ball into the air and see how many five times table facts your child can quickly call out while the ball is in the air.

Tables practice

1. Write in the missing answer to complete each multiplication fact.

$6 \times 5 = \boxed{}$ $1 \times 5 = \boxed{}$ $10 \times 5 = \boxed{}$

$3 \times 5 = \boxed{}$ $4 \times 5 = \boxed{}$ $5 \times 5 = \boxed{}$

$7 \times 5 = \boxed{}$ $12 \times 5 = \boxed{}$ $8 \times 5 = \boxed{}$

$9 \times 5 = \boxed{}$ $2 \times 5 = \boxed{}$ $11 \times 5 = \boxed{}$

2. Write in the missing number to complete each multiplication fact.

$\boxed{} \times 5 = 30$ $\boxed{} \times 5 = 20$ $\boxed{} \times 5 = 15$

$\boxed{} \times 5 = 5$ $\boxed{} \times 5 = 60$ $\boxed{} \times 5 = 45$

$\boxed{} \times 5 = 25$ $\boxed{} \times 5 = 35$ $\boxed{} \times 5 = 10$

$\boxed{} \times 5 = 50$ $\boxed{} \times 5 = 55$ $\boxed{} \times 5 = 40$

Activities

1. Count the tokens in each box. Each token is worth 5. Write a multiplication to show how much each box of tokens is worth.

$\boxed{} \times 5 = \boxed{}$ $\boxed{} \times \boxed{} = \boxed{}$ $\boxed{} \times \boxed{} = \boxed{}$

2. Draw a line to join each multiplication to its answer.

| 9 × 5 | 60 | | 15 | | 6 × 5 |

| 2 × 5 | 45 |

| 12 × 5 | | 3 × 5 |

| 10 | | 30 |

3. Each dart scores five times the number it lands on. Write the score for each dart in the box next to it.

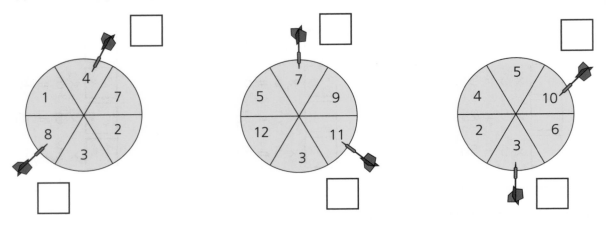

4. Each bar of chocolate has five pieces. Write a multiplication to show how many pieces of chocolate there are in each picture.

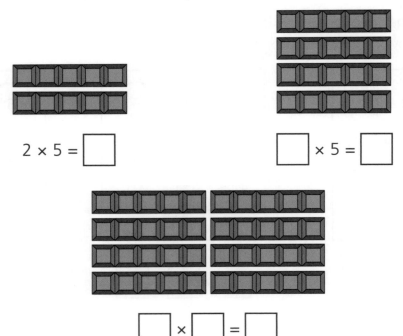

2 × 5 = ☐   ☐ × 5 = ☐

☐ × ☐ = ☐

5. Find a path through the maze. You may only go through numbers that are answers in the five times table.

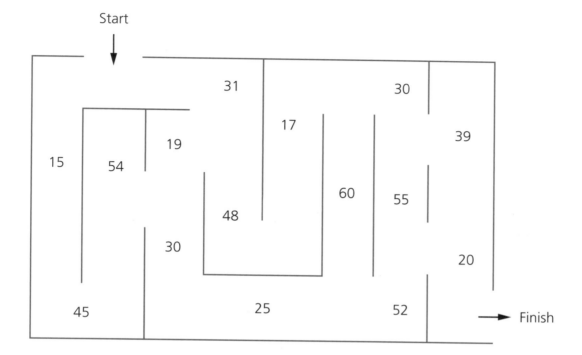

6. Draw a smiley face next to the tables facts with the correct answer.

Draw a sad face next to those with the wrong answer.

$3 \times 5 = 15$ ◯

$10 \times 5 = 50$ ◯

$7 \times 5 = 35$ ◯

$6 \times 5 = 25$ ◯

$9 \times 5 = 40$ ◯

$11 \times 5 = 55$ ◯

7. Complete the multiplication table.

	6	4	1	7	3	5	11
× 5							

8. Fill in the missing numbers by counting on or back in fives.

5	☐	15	☐	☐	☐	35
15	☐	☐	30	☐	☐	☐
35	30	☐	☐	☐	☐	5
60	55	☐	45	☐	☐	☐

9. This machine sorts numbers. Only numbers that are answers in the five times table go into the box below it. Write the numbers in the box.

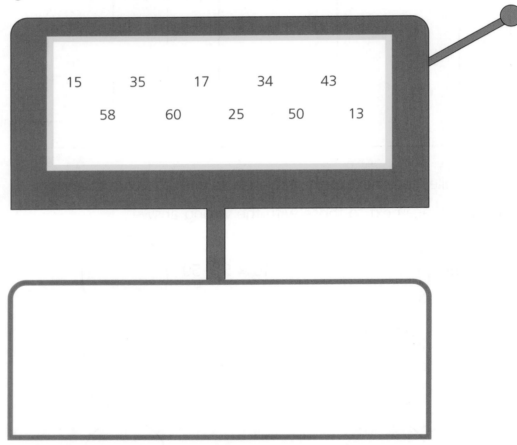

In the machine: 15   35   17   34   43   58   60   25   50   13

10. Write in the missing number to complete each multiplication fact.

35 = ☐ × 5   30 = ☐ × 5

15 = ☐ × 5   55 = ☐ × 5

10 = ☐ × 5   40 = ☐ × 5

Test your tables

1. Write out the five times table.

1 × 5 = ☐

2 × 5 = ☐

☐ × ☐ = ☐

☐ × ☐ = ☐

☐ × ☐ = ☐

☐ × ☐ = ☐

☐ × ☐ = ☐

☐ × ☐ = ☐

☐ × ☐ = ☐

☐ × ☐ = ☐

☐ × ☐ = ☐

☐ × ☐ = ☐

2. Complete these multiplication facts.

2 × 5 = ☐

☐ × 5 = 45

5 × 5 = ☐

☐ × 5 = 15

6 × 5 = ☐

8 × 5 = ☐

☐ × 5 = 20

☐ × 5 = 60

☐ × 5 = 35

11 × 5 = ☐

10 × 5 = ☐

☐ × 5 = 5

Score /12

Score /12

Four times table

Learn your tables

You can work out the answers to the four times table by doubling the two times table.

For example, 3 × 2 = **6** so double this to give 3 × 4 = **12**.

1	×	4	=	4
2	×	4	=	8
3	×	4	=	12
4	×	4	=	16
5	×	4	=	20
6	×	4	=	24
7	×	4	=	28
8	×	4	=	32
9	×	4	=	36
10	×	4	=	40
11	×	4	=	44
12	×	4	=	48

Parent's note

Make up a chant for a tables fact your child may struggle with. Here's an example:

"Knock, knock, who's at the gate, seven times four is twenty-eight."

As many animals have four legs, use them to help learn the four times table. Ask your child questions such as, "how many legs are there on four cats?"

Tables practice

1. Write in the missing answer to complete each multiplication fact.

$4 \times 4 = \boxed{}$ $2 \times 4 = \boxed{}$ $11 \times 4 = \boxed{}$

$8 \times 4 = \boxed{}$ $5 \times 4 = \boxed{}$ $1 \times 4 = \boxed{}$

$6 \times 4 = \boxed{}$ $10 \times 4 = \boxed{}$ $7 \times 4 = \boxed{}$

$12 \times 4 = \boxed{}$ $9 \times 4 = \boxed{}$ $3 \times 4 = \boxed{}$

2. Write in the missing number to complete each multiplication fact.

$\boxed{} \times 4 = 16$ $\boxed{} \times 4 = 12$ $\boxed{} \times 4 = 8$

$\boxed{} \times 4 = 28$ $\boxed{} \times 4 = 48$ $\boxed{} \times 4 = 44$

$\boxed{} \times 4 = 4$ $\boxed{} \times 4 = 20$ $\boxed{} \times 4 = 24$

$\boxed{} \times 4 = 40$ $\boxed{} \times 4 = 36$ $\boxed{} \times 4 = 32$

Activities

1. Fill in the grids by counting on or back in fours.

4			16				

12		20					40

40	36						

32	28				12		

Four times table

2. Find a path through the maze. You may only go through numbers that are answers in the four times table.

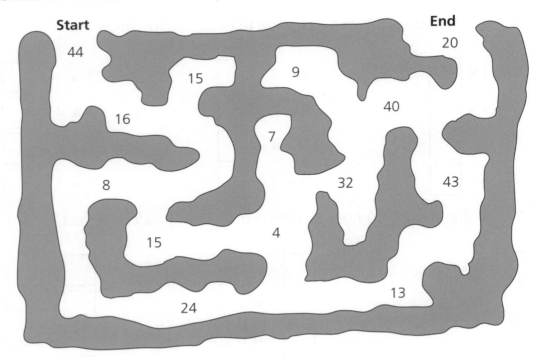

3. Here are some multiplications. Each one has the wrong answer. Write the correct answer in the box.

1 × 4 = 8 ☓ ☐   7 × 4 = 30 ☓ ☐

3 × 4 = 14 ☓ ☐   9 × 4 = 38 ☓ ☐

5 × 4 = 22 ☓ ☐   12 × 4 = 43 ☓ ☐

4. Draw a line to join each dog to the correct bone.

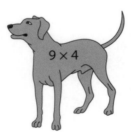  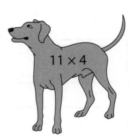 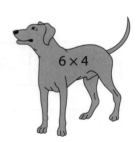

5. A four number code is needed to open the safe. The numbers are the answers to these tables facts.

3 × 4   8 × 4   12 × 4   5 × 4

Write the numbers in the safe.

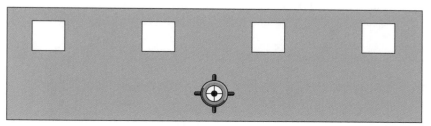

6. Complete the multiplication table.

× 4	5	3	1	8	11	2	6
		12					

7. Shade the correct multiplication for each answer.

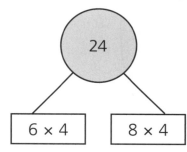
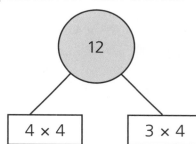
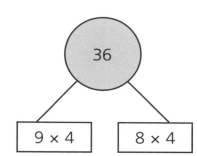

6 × 4	8 × 4		4 × 4	3 × 4		9 × 4	8 × 4

8. One sweet costs 4p.

4p each

Write down how many sweets you can buy with:

8p ☐   20p ☐   40p ☐

24p ☐   32p ☐   16p ☐

Four times table

9. Look at the numbers in the box. Circle the numbers that are answers in the four times table.

26	8	14	19
24	16	5	
38	32	10	12

10. Complete the multiplication wheel by writing the answers in the boxes.

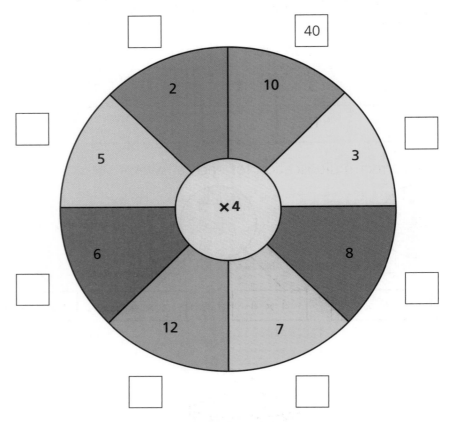

11. Colour the blocks in the wall that contain answers in the four times table.

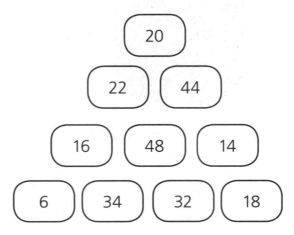

Test your tables

1. Write out the four times table.

$$1 \times 4 = \boxed{}$$

$$2 \times 4 = \boxed{}$$

$$\boxed{} \times \boxed{} = \boxed{}$$

$$\boxed{} \times \boxed{} = \boxed{}$$

$$\boxed{} \times \boxed{} = \boxed{}$$

$$\boxed{} \times \boxed{} = \boxed{}$$

$$\boxed{} \times \boxed{} = \boxed{}$$

$$\boxed{} \times \boxed{} = \boxed{}$$

$$\boxed{} \times \boxed{} = \boxed{}$$

$$\boxed{} \times \boxed{} = \boxed{}$$

$$\boxed{} \times \boxed{} = \boxed{}$$

2. Complete these multiplication facts.

$$3 \times 4 = \boxed{}$$

$$\boxed{} \times 4 = 8$$

$$5 \times 4 = \boxed{}$$

$$\boxed{} \times 4 = 24$$

$$8 \times 4 = \boxed{}$$

$$9 \times 4 = \boxed{}$$

$$\boxed{} \times 4 = 16$$

$$\boxed{} \times 4 = 48$$

$$\boxed{} \times 4 = 28$$

$$1 \times 4 = \boxed{}$$

$$11 \times 4 = \boxed{}$$

$$\boxed{} \times 4 = 40$$

Score   /12

Score   /12

Learn your tables

The answers to the three times table swap between odd and even.

An odd number ends in 1, 3, 5, 7, or 9.

An even number ends in 0, 2, 4, 6 or 8.

$$1 \times 3 = 3$$
$$2 \times 3 = 6$$
$$3 \times 3 = 9$$
$$4 \times 3 = 12$$
$$5 \times 3 = 15$$
$$6 \times 3 = 18$$
$$7 \times 3 = 21$$
$$8 \times 3 = 24$$
$$9 \times 3 = 27$$
$$10 \times 3 = 30$$
$$11 \times 3 = 33$$
$$12 \times 3 = 36$$

Parent's note

It may be helpful to learn a times table in chunks rather than all in one go, for example, four facts at a time.

Use household items such as buttons, beads and pencils to make arrays to show some tables facts, for example, four rows of three buttons to show 4 × 3 = 12.

One times table

Tables practice

1. 5, 12, 3, 7, 4, 8, 1, 11, 2, 9, 10, 6

2. 4, 6, 11, 2, 7, 1, 5, 3, 8, 10, 12, 9

Activities

1. 2 × 1 and 2, 4 × 1 and 4, 6 × 1 and 6, 9 × 1 and 9, 3 × 1 and 3

2. 2, 5, 10, 12, 3, 6

Two times table

Tables practice

1. 24, 10, 6, 2, 20, 22, 18, 4, 12, 14, 8, 16

2. 7, 3, 4, 1, 6, 11, 5, 2, 9, 10, 8, 12

Activities

1. 4 × 2 = 8, 3 × 2 = 6, 7 × 2 = 14, 2 × 2 = 4

2. 4 × 2 = 8, 8 × 2 = 16, 6 × 2 = 12

3. 7 × 2 = 14, 2 × 2 = 4, 8 × 2 = 16, 3 × 2 = 6, 9 × 2 = 18, 11 × 2 = 22

4. Circle 9 × 2, 4 × 2, 6 × 2, 12 × 2

5. Colour 4, 12, 8, 22, 20, 6, 16; Scooter

6. 10, 6, 18, 24

7. Shade 12, 2, 6, 18, 4, 8, 22, 24, 16, 10

8. 6, 16, 18, 12, 4, 22

9. 6 × 2 = 12 (purple), 5 × 2 = 10 (black), 9 × 2 = 18 (grey), 11 × 2 = 22 (yellow), 7 × 2 = 14 (blue), 3 × 2 = 6 (red)

10. Circle 20, 6, 22, 4, 18, 12

Test your tables

1. 1 × 2 = 2, 2 × 2 = 4, 3 × 2 = 6, 4 × 2 = 8, 5 × 2 = 10, 6 × 2 = 12, 7 × 2 = 14, 8 × 2 = 16, 9 × 2 = 18, 10 × 2 = 20, 11 × 2 = 22, 12 × 2 = 24

2. 6 × 2 = 12, 12 × 2 = 24, 9 × 2 = 18, 4 × 2 = 8, 1 × 2 = 2, 8 × 2 = 16, 7 × 2 = 14, 2 × 2 = 4, 11 × 2 = 22, 3 × 2 = 6, 5 × 2 = 10, 10 × 2 = 20

Ten times table

Tables practice

1. 40, 120, 20, 70, 30, 80, 10, 90, 100, 50, 110, 60

2. 5, 12, 11, 8, 7, 9, 1, 10, 6, 3, 2, 4

Activities

1. 8 × 10 = 80, 6 × 10 = 60, 7 × 10 = 70, 4 × 10 = 40, 1 × 10 = 10, 5 × 10 = 50, 9 × 10 = 90

2. 4 × 10 = 40, 12 × 10 = 120, 5 × 10 = 50, 7 × 10 = 70

3. 3 × 10 = 30, 6 × 10 = 60, 8 × 10 = 80, 11 × 10 = 110

4. 2, 5, 4, 8, 3, 12

5. 3 × 10 = 30, 9 × 10 = 90, 12 × 10 = 120, 4 × 10 = 40, 8 × 10 = 80

6. 30, 10, 20, 70, 120, 50

7. 30, 50, 60, 70, 80;
70, 80, 90, 100, 110;
60, 50, 40, 30;
110, 90, 80, 70, 60

8. 3 × 10 = 30, 5 × 10 = 50, 6 × 10 = 60, 11 × 10 = 110, 9 × 10 = 90

9. 5 × 10 = 50, 8 × 10 = 80, 11 × 10 = 110, 2 × 10 = 20, 4 × 10 = 40, 10 × 10 = 100, 9 × 10 = 90, 1 × 10 = 10

10. Circle 10 × 10, 8 × 10, 7 × 10, 9 × 10

Test your tables

1. 1 × 10 = 10, 2 × 10 = 20, 3 × 10 = 30, 4 × 10 = 40, 5 × 10 = 50, 6 × 10 = 60, 7 × 10 = 70, 8 × 10 = 80, 9 × 10 = 90, 10 × 10 = 100, 11 × 10 = 110, 12 × 10 = 120

2. 4 × 10 = 40, 7 × 10 = 70, 1 × 10 = 10, 12 × 10 = 120, 5 × 10 = 50, 6 × 10 = 60, 8 × 10 = 80, 2 × 10 = 20, 10 × 10 = 100, 3 × 10 = 30, 11 × 10 = 110, 9 × 10 = 90

Five times table

Tables practice

1. 30, 5, 50, 15, 20, 25, 35, 60, 40, 45, 10, 55

2. 6, 4, 3, 1, 12, 9, 5, 7, 2, 10, 11, 8

Activities

1. 5 × 5 = 25, 8 × 5 = 40, 7 × 5 = 35

2. 9 × 5 = 45, 6 × 5 = 30, 2 × 5 = 10, 12 × 5 = 60, 3 × 5 = 15

3. First board (from top): 20, 40;

Answers

Second board (from top): 35, 55;
Third board (from top): 50, 15

4. 2 × 5 = 10, 4 × 5 = 20, 8 × 5 = 40

5. Path drawn through: 15, 45, 30, 25, 60, 30, 55, 20

6. smiley, smiley, smiley, sad, sad, smiley

7. 30, 20, 5, 35, 15, 25, 55

8. 10, 20, 25, 30;
20, 25, 35, 40, 45;
25, 20, 15, 10;
50, 40, 35, 30

9. 15, 35, 60, 25, 50

10. 7, 6, 3, 11, 2, 8

Test your tables

1. 1 × 5 = 5, 2 × 5 = 10, 3 × 5 = 15,
4 × 5 = 20, 5 × 5 = 25, 6 × 5 = 30,
7 × 5 = 35, 8 × 5 = 40, 9 × 5 = 45,
10 × 5 = 50, 11 × 5 = 55, 12 × 5 = 60

2. 2 × 5 = 10, 9 × 5 = 45, 5 × 5 = 25,
3 × 5 = 15, 6 × 5 = 30, 8 × 5 = 40,
4 × 5 = 20, 12 × 5 = 60, 7 × 5 = 35,
11 × 5 = 55, 10 × 5 = 50, 1 × 5 = 5

Four times tables

Tables practice

1. 16, 8, 44, 32, 20, 4, 24, 40, 28, 48, 36, 12

2. 4, 3, 2, 7, 12, 11, 1, 5, 6, 10, 9, 8

Activities

1. 8, 12, 20, 24, 28, 32;
16, 24, 28, 32, 36;
32, 28, 24, 20, 16, 12;
24, 20, 16, 8, 4

2. Path drawn through: 44, 16, 8, 24, 4, 32, 40, 20

3. 4, 28, 12, 36, 20, 48

4. 9 × 4 = 36, 3 × 4 = 12, 11 × 4 = 44,
6 × 4 = 24

5. 12, 32, 48, 20

6. 20, 4, 32, 44, 8, 24

7. Shade 6 × 4, 3 × 4, 9 × 4

8. 2, 5, 10, 6, 8, 4

9. Circle 8, 24, 16, 32, 12

10. Clockwise from '40': 12, 32, 28, 48, 24, 20, 8

11. Colour 20, 44, 16, 48, 32

Test your tables

1. 1 × 4 = 4, 2 × 4 = 8, 3 × 4 = 12,
4 × 4 = 16, 5 × 4 = 20, 6 × 4 = 24,
7 × 4 = 28, 8 × 4 = 32, 9 × 4 = 36,
10 × 4 = 40, 11 × 4 = 44, 12 × 4 = 48

2. 3 × 4 = 12, 2 × 4 = 8, 5 × 4 = 20,
6 × 4 = 24, 8 × 4 = 32, 9 × 4 = 36,
4 × 4 = 16, 12 × 4 = 48, 7 × 4 = 28,
1 × 4 = 4, 11 × 4 = 44, 10 × 4 = 40

Three times table

Tables practice

1. 15, 12, 27, 24, 30, 33, 36, 9, 6, 18, 21, 3

2. 6, 3, 2, 1, 11, 9, 4, 5, 10, 8, 12, 7

Activities

1. 36, 3, 15, 24, 18

2. First snake: 18, 15, 9, 3; First ladder:
15, 21, 24, 27, 33; Second snake: 24, 18,
15, 12, 6; Second ladder: 18, 21, 24,
27, 30

3. 18, 9, 15, 6, 36, 21, 27

4. Colour 6, 33, 24

5. First board (clockwise from '12'): 3, 21, 33,
15, 24; Second board (clockwise from top):
6, 18, 9, 36, 30, 27

6. 3 × 3 and 9, 4 × 3 and 12, 8 × 3 and 24,
5 × 3 and 15

7. Colour 3, 6, 9, 12, 15, 18, 21, 24, 27, 30;
The answers lie on diagonal lines.

8. 5, 3, 8, 1, 4, 12, 11, 2, 6

9. Circle 6 × 3, 3 × 3, 9 × 3, 10 × 3

10. smiley, sad, sad, smiley, smiley, smiley

Test your tables

1. 1 × 3 = 3, 2 × 3 = 6, 3 × 3 = 9,
4 × 3 = 12, 5 × 3 = 15, 6 × 3 = 18,
7 × 3 = 21, 8 × 3 = 24, 9 × 3 = 27,
10 × 3 = 30, 11 × 3 = 33, 12 × 3 = 36

2. 1 × 3 = 3, 9 × 3 = 27, 3 × 3 = 9,
4 × 3 = 12, 7 × 3 = 21, 10 × 3 = 30,
5 × 3 = 15, 12 × 3 = 36, 11 × 3 = 33,
8 × 3 = 24, 2 × 3 = 6, 6 × 3 = 18

Five and ten times tables

Tables practice

1. $1 \times 5 = 5$, $2 \times 5 = 10$, $3 \times 5 = 15$, $4 \times 5 = 20$, $5 \times 5 = 25$, $6 \times 5 = 30$, $7 \times 5 = 35$, $8 \times 5 = 40$, $9 \times 5 = 45$, $10 \times 5 = 50$, $11 \times 5 = 55$, $12 \times 5 = 60$

2. $1 \times 10 = 10$, $2 \times 10 = 20$, $3 \times 10 = 30$, $4 \times 10 = 40$, $5 \times 10 = 50$, $6 \times 10 = 60$, $7 \times 10 = 70$, $8 \times 10 = 80$, $9 \times 10 = 90$, $10 \times 10 = 100$, $11 \times 10 = 110$, $12 \times 10 = 120$

3. 60, 1, 30, 3, 25, 9, 50, 80, 7, 6, 40, 5, 6, 55, 10, 20, 2, 70, 12, 20, 2, 40, 45, 11

Activities

1. (×5) 5 30, 20, 60, 15, 35, 5; (×10) 60, 40, 120, 30, 70, 10
2. 15, 90, 110, 25, 10, 50
3. 8, 9, 3, 3, 7, 11, 8, 4, 12
4. Path drawn through: 15, 30, 70, 25, 90, 45, 110, 20
5. 10, 5, 4, 2, 12, 6
6. Circle 25, 70, 45, 20
7. £30, £30, £120, £20, £20, £35; 5, 5
8. First board: $8 \times 5 = 40$, $6 \times 10 = 60$, $12 \times 5 = 60$; Second board: $4 \times 5 = 20$, $11 \times 5 = 55$, $9 \times 10 = 90$
9. 2, 12, 4, 6; 1, 6, 2, 3

Two and four times tables

Tables practice

1. $1 \times 2 = 2$, $2 \times 2 = 4$, $3 \times 2 = 6$, $4 \times 2 = 8$, $5 \times 2 = 10$, $6 \times 2 = 12$, $7 \times 2 = 14$, $8 \times 2 = 16$, $9 \times 2 = 18$, $10 \times 2 = 20$, $11 \times 2 = 22$, $12 \times 2 = 24$

2. $1 \times 4 = 4$, $2 \times 4 = 8$, $3 \times 4 = 12$, $4 \times 4 = 16$, $5 \times 4 = 20$, $6 \times 4 = 24$, $7 \times 4 = 28$, $8 \times 4 = 32$, $9 \times 4 = 36$, $10 \times 4 = 40$, $11 \times 4 = 44$, $12 \times 4 = 48$

3. 8, 8, 16, 2, 10, 9, 12, 4, 3, 4, 12, 40, 12, 44, 6, 28, 18, 6, 10, 16, 14, 1, 22, 5

Activities

1. (×2) 22, 14, 16, 6, 18, 4; (×4) 44, 28, 32, 12, 36, 8
2. Red circle – 4, 2, 18, 6, 16, 22, 24, 20; Blue square – 4, 16, 24, 20; Both – 4, 16, 24, 20
3. First machine: 4, 12, 14, 24; Second machine: 8, 24, 28, 48 The numbers coming out of the second machine are double the numbers coming out of the first.
4. 20, 8, 24, 36
5. 14, 16, 18, 22, 24; 14, 12, 10, 8, 6, 4; 28, 32, 36, 40, 48; 28, 24, 20, 16, 12, 8
6. Shade 16, 4, 36, 8, 12, 18, 2, 28, 6, 10, 44
7. 2, 6, 8, 12, 16, 18, 22, 24, 32
8. circle

Two, three and ten times tables

Activities

1. (×2) 6, 22, 8, 2, 18, 24, 10; (×3) 9, 33, 12, 3, 27, 36, 15; (×10) 30, 110, 40, 10, 90, 120, 50
2. 6, 3, 4
3. First board (clockwise from top): 14, 120, 27; Second board (clockwise from top): 6, 15, 40; Third board (clockwise from top): 4, 30, 110
4. Twos: 6, 8, 10, 14, 16, 18, 22; Threes: 18, 21, 24, 27, 30, 36; Tens: 10, 30
5. sad, smiley, smiley, sad, smiley, smiley, sad, sad
6. Pink bow tie: $3 \times 2 = 6$, $2 \times 3 = 6$, Blue tie: $7 \times 3 = 21$, Red tie: $5 \times 10 = 50$, Yellow bow tie: $6 \times 3 = 18$, $9 \times 2 = 18$
7. 12, 15, 18, 21, 24, 27, 30
8. Path drawn through: 12, 3, 20, 50, 18, 21, 24, 60, 9, 90
9. 6, 10, 7, 2, 7, 4, 8, 5, 2, 10, 1, 12
10. Two only – 14, 22; Three only – 15, 21, 9, 33; Both – 6, 24, 12

Answers

11. Twos – 4, 6, 8, 10, 14, 16, 18;
Threes – 6, 9, 15, 18, 21, 27, 30;
Tens – 20, 30, 40, 60, 70, 80, 100

Three, four and five times tables

Activities

1. (×3) 18, 21, 15, 33, 9, 30, 24;
(×4) 24, 28, 20, 44, 12, 40, 32;
(×5) 30, 35, 25, 55, 15, 50, 40

2. £18, £9, £24, £20, £5, £21, £20, £60

3. Circle 40, 36, 21, 48

4. 5, 10, 7, 9, 7, 12, 3, 2, 5, 11, 4, 8

5. 15, 18, 21, 35, 40

6. 6 × 4 and 8 × 3, 12 × 3 and 9 × 4, 10 × 3 and 6 × 5

7. 3, 6, 10, 9, 6

8. Three only – 18, 33, 3; Four only – 32, 16, 20, 28; Both – 24, 36, 12

9. 15, 25, 30, 40, 45;
24, 28, 36, 40, 44;
30, 27, 21, 18, 15, 12;
50, 45, 40, 35, 30, 25, 20

10. First wheel (clockwise from top): 12, 8, 36, 8, 28, 10; Second wheel (clockwise from top): 1, 55, 15, 6, 40, 35

11. Red circle – 3, 6, 9, 12, 15, 18, 21, 24, 27, 30;
Blue circle – 4, 8, 12, 16, 20, 24, 28;
Green circle – 5, 10, 15, 20, 25, 30;
Circled twice – 12, 15, 20, 24, 30

12. smiley, smiley, sad, sad, sad, smiley

Mixed times tables

Activities

1. 45, 10, 24, 28, 22, 30; penguin

2. Clockwise from the top: 120, 20, 44, 27, 4

3. 2, 10, 8;
3, 6, 8

4. 2 × 10 = 20, 2 × 5 = 10,
3 × 10 = 30, 3 × 5 = 15,
4 × 10 = 40, 4 × 5 = 20,
5 × 10 = 50, 5 × 5 = 25,
6 × 10 = 60, 6 × 5 = 30

5. 2 × 2 = 4, 2 × 4 = 8,
3 × 2 = 6, 3 × 4 = 12,
4 × 2 = 8, 4 × 4 = 16,
5 × 2 = 10, 5 × 4 = 20,
6 × 2 = 12, 6 × 4 = 24

6. 2, 4, 6, 8, 10;
3, 6, 9, 12, 15;
4, 8, 12, 16, 20

7. Circle 18, 4, 35, 12, 100

8. 9, 9, 7, 3, 12, 1, 1, 5, 3, 8, 9, 12

9. Colour 8, 15, 9, 3, 32, 27, 16, 21, 20, 24, 6; flower pot

10. 10, 10, 10, 10;
30, 30, 30;
24, 24, 24; Each set has the same answer

11. smiley, sad, smiley, smiley, sad, sad

12. Shade 36, 21, 16, 8, 25, 35, 24, 32, 40; Letter 'X'

Speed tests

Test 1

16, 24, 18, 110, 60, 60, 40, 25, 4, 28, 21, 30, 8, 10, 12, 45, 6, 15, 100, 7, 2, 15, 20, 12, 50, 9, 5, 9, 30, 8, 6, 44, 12, 50, 22, 30, 40, 18, 80, 10

Test 2

35, 20, 32, 120, 8, 4, 40, 10, 55, 16, 90, 27, 33, 20, 24, 36, 48, 3, 20, 70, 6, 30, 36, 6, 16, 20, 28, 60, 10, 10, 4, 15, 45, 24, 16, 50, 33, 50, 30, 120

Multiplication grids

Grid 1

1	2	3	4	5	10
2	4	6	8	10	20
3	6	9	12	15	30
4	8	12	16	20	40
5	10	15	20	25	50
6	12	18	24	30	60
7	14	21	28	35	70
8	16	24	32	40	80
9	18	27	36	45	90
10	20	30	40	50	100
11	22	33	44	55	110
12	24	36	48	60	120

Grid 2

8	12	16	20	40
12	18	24	30	60
22	33	44	55	110
4	6	8	10	20
24	36	48	60	120
18	27	36	45	90
10	15	20	25	50
2	3	4	5	10
6	9	12	15	30
14	21	28	35	70
20	30	40	50	100
16	24	32	40	80

Tables practice

1. Write in the missing answer to complete each multiplication fact.

5 × 3 = ☐   4 × 3 = ☐   9 × 3 = ☐

8 × 3 = ☐   10 × 3 = ☐   11 × 3 = ☐

12 × 3 = ☐   3 × 3 = ☐   2 × 3 = ☐

6 × 3 = ☐   7 × 3 = ☐   1 × 3 = ☐

2. Write in the missing number to complete each multiplication fact.

☐ × 3 = 18   ☐ × 3 = 9   ☐ × 3 = 6

☐ × 3 = 3   ☐ × 3 = 33   ☐ × 3 = 27

☐ × 3 = 12   ☐ × 3 = 15   ☐ × 3 = 30

☐ × 3 = 24   ☐ × 3 = 36   ☐ × 3 = 21

Activities

1. This machine sorts numbers. Only numbers that are answers in the three times table go into the box below it. Write the numbers in the box.

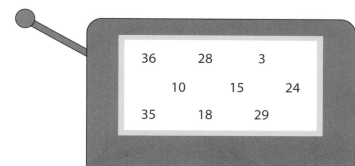

36   28   3
10   15   24
35   18   29

Three times table

2. Count on in threes on each ladder.

Count back in threes on each snake.

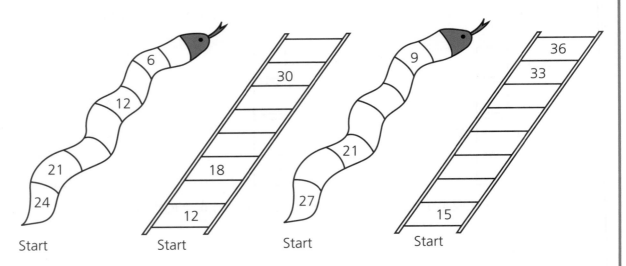

3. Complete the multiplication table.

	6	3	5	2	12	7	9
× 3							

4. Only the boxes with an answer in the three times table have treasure in them. Colour these boxes.

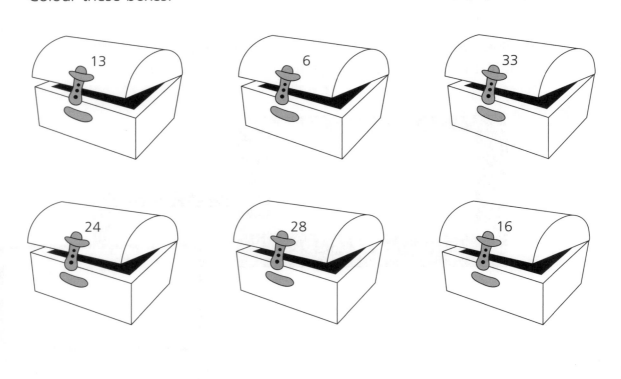

5. Complete the target boards using the three times table.

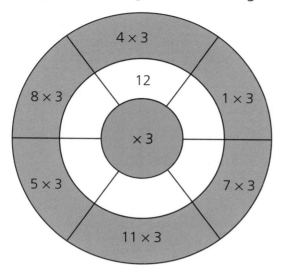 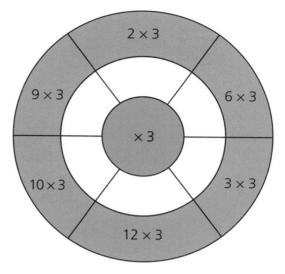

6. Draw a string from each kite to the correct answer.

 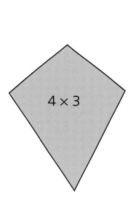  

| 12 | | 9 | | 15 | | 24 |

7. Colour in the numbers that are answers in the three times table.

What pattern can you see? _____

1	2	3	4	5	6	7	8	9	10
11	12	13	14	15	16	17	18	19	20
21	22	23	24	25	26	27	28	29	30

Three times table

8. Write in the missing number to complete each multiplication fact.

15 = ☐ × 3   9 = ☐ × 3   24 = ☐ × 3

3 = ☐ × 3   12 = ☐ × 3   36 = ☐ × 3

33 = ☐ × 3   6 = ☐ × 3   18 = ☐ × 3

9. Circle the multiplication that matches the number in the box.

18	4 × 3	6 × 3	10 × 3	7 × 3
9	3 × 3	4 × 3	6 × 3	8 × 3
27	8 × 3	5 × 3	9 × 3	2 × 3
30	11 × 3	10 × 3	12 × 3	6 × 3

10. Draw a smiley face next to the tables facts with the correct answer.

Draw a sad face next to those with the wrong answer.

2 × 3 = 6 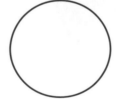   10 × 3 = 28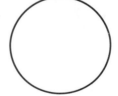

4 × 3 = 14    1 × 3 = 3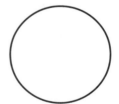

6 × 3 = 18    11 × 3 = 33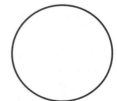

Test your tables

1. Write out the three times table.

1 × 3 = ☐

2 × 3 = ☐

☐ × ☐ = ☐

☐ × ☐ = ☐

☐ × ☐ = ☐

☐ × ☐ = ☐

☐ × ☐ = ☐

☐ × ☐ = ☐

☐ × ☐ = ☐

☐ × ☐ = ☐

☐ × ☐ = ☐

☐ × ☐ = ☐

2. Complete these multiplication facts.

☐ × 3 = 3

9 × 3 = ☐

3 × 3 = ☐

☐ × 3 = 12

7 × 3 = ☐

☐ × 3 = 30

5 × 3 = ☐

12 × 3 = ☐

☐ × 3 = 33

☐ × 3 = 24

2 × 3 = ☐

☐ × 3 = 18

Score /12

Score /12

Five and ten times tables

1. Write out the five times table as quickly as you can.

$1 \times 5 = \boxed{}$ $2 \times 5 = \boxed{}$ $\boxed{} \times \boxed{} = \boxed{}$

$\boxed{} \times \boxed{} = \boxed{}$ $\boxed{} \times \boxed{} = \boxed{}$ $\boxed{} \times \boxed{} = \boxed{}$

$\boxed{} \times \boxed{} = \boxed{}$ $\boxed{} \times \boxed{} = \boxed{}$ $\boxed{} \times \boxed{} = \boxed{}$

$\boxed{} \times \boxed{} = \boxed{}$ $\boxed{} \times \boxed{} = \boxed{}$ $\boxed{} \times \boxed{} = \boxed{}$

2. Write out the ten times table as quickly as you can.

$1 \times 10 = \boxed{}$ $2 \times 10 = \boxed{}$ $\boxed{} \times \boxed{} = \boxed{}$

$\boxed{} \times \boxed{} = \boxed{}$ $\boxed{} \times \boxed{} = \boxed{}$ $\boxed{} \times \boxed{} = \boxed{}$

$\boxed{} \times \boxed{} = \boxed{}$ $\boxed{} \times \boxed{} = \boxed{}$ $\boxed{} \times \boxed{} = \boxed{}$

$\boxed{} \times \boxed{} = \boxed{}$ $\boxed{} \times \boxed{} = \boxed{}$ $\boxed{} \times \boxed{} = \boxed{}$

3. Write in the missing number to complete each multiplication fact.

$12 \times 5 = \boxed{}$ $\boxed{} \times 10 = 10$ $3 \times 10 = \boxed{}$

$\boxed{} \times 5 = 15$ $5 \times 5 = \boxed{}$ $\boxed{} \times 10 = 90$

$5 \times 10 = \boxed{}$ $8 \times 10 = \boxed{}$ $\boxed{} \times 5 = 35$

$\boxed{} \times 5 = 30$ $8 \times 5 = \boxed{}$ $1 \times 5 = \boxed{}$

$\boxed{} \times 10 = 60$ $11 \times 5 = \boxed{}$ $\boxed{} \times 10 = 100$

$4 \times 5 = \boxed{}$ $\boxed{} \times 5 = 10$ $7 \times 10 = \boxed{}$

$\boxed{} \times 10 = 120$ $2 \times 10 = \boxed{}$ $\boxed{} \times 10 = 20$

$4 \times 10 = \boxed{}$ $9 \times 5 = \boxed{}$ $\boxed{} \times 10 = 110$

Activities

1. Complete the multiplication grid for the five and ten times tables.

×	6	4	12	3	7	1
5						
10						

2. This machine sorts numbers. Only numbers that are answers in the five or tens times tables go into the box below it. Write the numbers in the box.

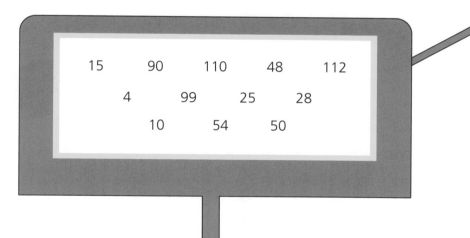

3. Write in the missing number to complete each multiplication fact.

80 = ☐ × 10   45 = ☐ × 5   30 = ☐ × 10

15 = ☐ × 5   70 = ☐ × 10   55 = ☐ × 5

40 = ☐ × 5   40 = ☐ × 10   120 = ☐ × 10

Five and ten times tables

4. The frog must find a path to the pond. It must only pass through numbers that are answers in the five or ten times tables. Draw the path the frog must take.

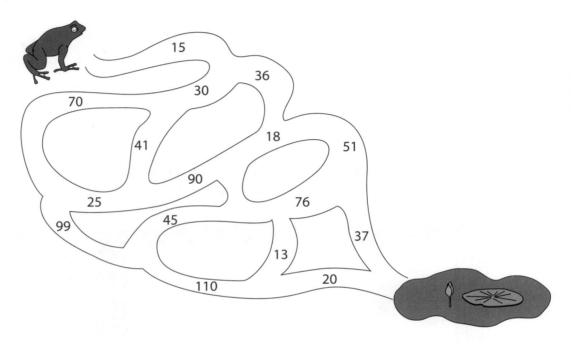

5. Complete the two tables facts that give the answer in the star.

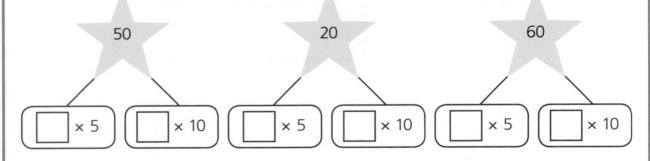

6. Circle the correct answer for the multiplication in each box.

5 × 5	35	45	25	15
7 × 10	80	50	75	70
9 × 5	45	90	55	35
2 × 10	30	25	20	40

7. A book costs £10 and a game costs £5.

Write down how much it costs for:

3 books   £ ☐   6 games   £ ☐   12 books   £ ☐

4 games   £ ☐   2 books   £ ☐   7 games   £ ☐

How many games can you buy for £25? ☐

How many books can you buy for £50? ☐

8. Each arrow scores five or ten times the number on it. Write out and complete the multiplications to show the score for each arrow.

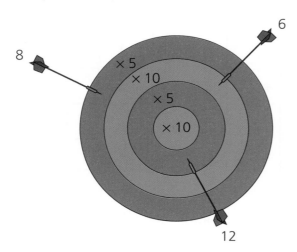
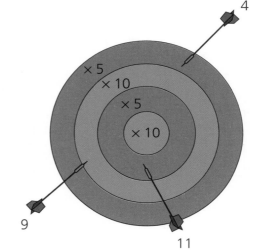

8 × 5 = ☐   4 × ☐ = ☐

6 × ☐ = ☐   11 × ☐ = ☐

12 × ☐ = ☐   9 × ☐ = ☐

9. An apple costs 10p, a pineapple costs 60p, a banana costs 20p and a coconut costs 30p.

How many coins would you need to buy each fruit if you can only use 5p or 10p coins?

	apple	pineapple	banana	coconut
5p coins only	☐	☐	☐	☐
10p coins only	☐	☐	☐	☐

Two and four times tables

1. Write out the two times table as quickly as you can.

1 × 2 = ☐

☐ × ☐ = ☐

☐ × ☐ = ☐

☐ × ☐ = ☐

2 × 2 = ☐

☐ × ☐ = ☐

☐ × ☐ = ☐

☐ × ☐ = ☐

☐ × ☐ = ☐

☐ × ☐ = ☐

☐ × ☐ = ☐

☐ × ☐ = ☐

2. Write out the four times table as quickly as you can.

1 × 4 = ☐

☐ × ☐ = ☐

☐ × ☐ = ☐

☐ × ☐ = ☐

2 × 4 = ☐

☐ × ☐ = ☐

☐ × ☐ = ☐

☐ × ☐ = ☐

☐ × ☐ = ☐

☐ × ☐ = ☐

☐ × ☐ = ☐

☐ × ☐ = ☐

3. Write in the missing number to complete each multiplication fact.

4 × 2 = ☐

☐ × 4 = 8

3 × 4 = ☐

2 × 2 = ☐

☐ × 4 = 48

7 × 4 = ☐

☐ × 2 = 20

☐ × 2 = 2

☐ × 4 = 32

5 × 2 = ☐

1 × 4 = ☐

☐ × 2 = 24

11 × 4 = ☐

9 × 2 = ☐

8 × 2 = ☐

11 × 2 = ☐

4 × 4 = ☐

☐ × 4 = 36

☐ × 2 = 6

10 × 4 = ☐

☐ × 2 = 12

☐ × 4 = 24

7 × 2 = ☐

☐ × 4 = 20

Two and four times tables

Activities

1. Complete the multiplication grid for the two and four times tables.

×	11	7	8	3	9	2
2						
4						

2. Draw a red circle around the numbers that are answers in the two times table.

   Draw a blue square around the numbers that are answers in the four times table.

4	23	2	18
6	16	11	21
22	24	7	20

Which numbers are answers in both the two and four times tables?

_____

3. Here are two number machines. Write in the missing numbers.

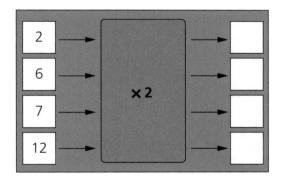 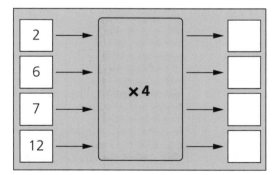

What do you notice about the numbers coming out of the two machines?

_____

_____

Two and four times tables

4. An elephant has four legs.

Write down how many legs there are on:

5 elephants ☐   2 elephants ☐

6 elephants ☐   9 elephants ☐

5. Fill in the missing numbers by counting on or back in twos or fours.

10	12	☐	☐	☐	20	☐	☐
18	16	☐	☐	☐	☐	☐	☐
20	24	☐	☐	☐	☐	44	☐
36	32	☐	☐	☐	☐	☐	☐

6. Shade a path through the number grid. Only shade answers that are in the two or four times tables.

27	3	45	35	43	44	→ End
11	37	13	33	6	10	
25	7	47	2	28	9	
21	19	12	18	17	49	
5	23	8	39	41	31	
16	4	36	1	15	29	

Start →

7. The straight path follows the four times table. The curved path follows the two times table. Write in the missing numbers.

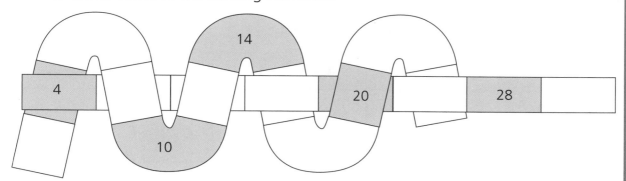

8. For each row, there is one tables fact that is correct and one that is wrong. Colour in yellow the circle next to the correct tables fact.

2 × 4 = 8 c   2 × 4 = 10 t

6 × 2 = 10 p   6 × 2 = 12 i

12 × 4 = 48 r   12 × 4 = 4 m

8 × 2 = 18 b   8 × 2 = 16 c

9 × 4 = 36 l   9 × 4 = 38 q

12 × 2 = 26 f   12 × 2 = 24 e

Write the yellow letters in the space below.

The name of the shape is _____.

Two, three and ten times tables

Activities

1. Complete the multiplication grid.

×	3	11	4	1	9	12	5
2							
3							
10							

2. Here is the price list for an ice-cream parlour.

Single cone	£2
Double cone	£3
Giant sundae	£10

How many single cones can be bought with £12? ☐

How many double cones can be bought with £9? ☐

How many giant sundaes can be bought with £40? ☐

3. Each arrow scores two, three or ten times the number on it. Write the score for each arrow in the box next to it.

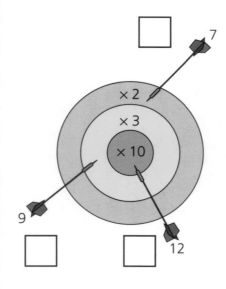

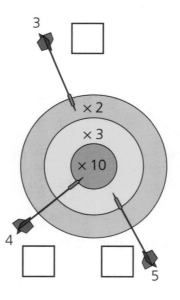

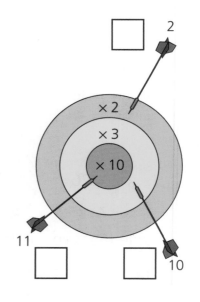

44

Two, three and ten times tables

4. Complete the puzzle by counting in twos, threes and tens.

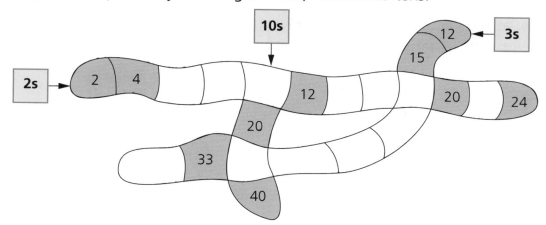

5. Draw a smiley face next to the tables facts with the correct answer.

Draw a sad face next to those with the wrong answer.

7 × 3 = 24 ◯   2 × 3 = 6 ◯

4 × 4 = 16 ◯   5 × 3 = 16 ◯

9 × 10 = 90 ◯   8 × 4 = 32 ◯

5 × 10 = 60 ◯   6 × 4 = 26 ◯

6. Complete the multiplications on each tie and bow-tie to make the answer in the knot.

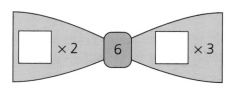

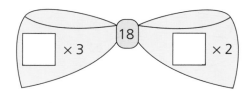

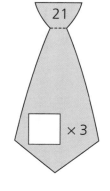

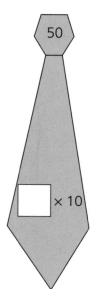

Two, three and ten times tables

7. Have you noticed that each of your thumbs and fingers have three parts?

Look at the picture below to see how you can use your hands to help you with the three times table. Fill in the missing numbers in the three times table.

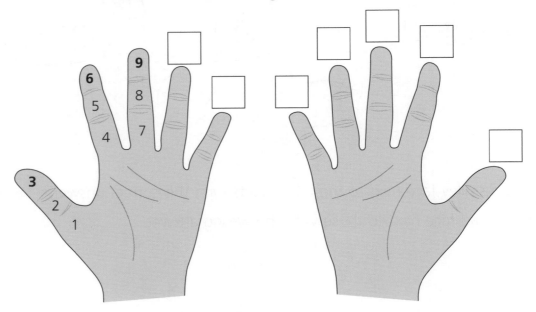

8. Find a path out of the castle through the maze. You may only go through numbers that are answers in the two, three or ten times tables.

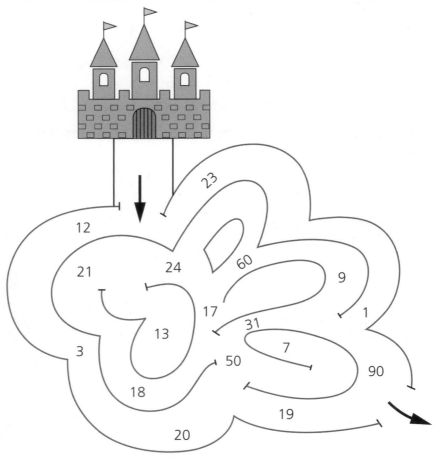

9. Write in the number to complete each multiplication.

18 = ☐ × 3   100 = ☐ × 10   14 = ☐ × 2

6 = ☐ × 3   70 = ☐ × 10   8 = ☐ × 2

24 = ☐ × 3   50 = ☐ × 10   4 = ☐ × 2

30 = ☐ × 3   10 = ☐ × 10   24 = ☐ × 2

10. This machine sorts numbers. Sort the numbers into those that are answers in the two times table only, those that are in the three times table only and those that are in both.

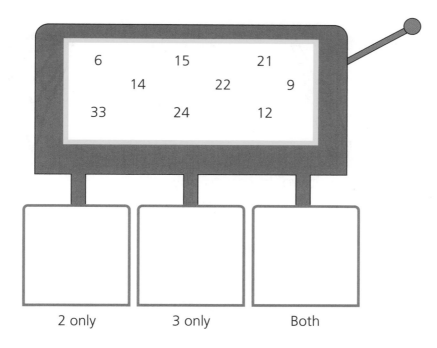

6   15   21

14   22   9

33   24   12

2 only   3 only   Both

11. Count on in twos, threes and tens.

2   ☐ ☐ ☐ ☐   12   ☐ ☐ ☐   20

3   ☐ ☐   12   ☐ ☐ ☐   24   ☐ ☐

10   ☐ ☐ ☐   50   ☐ ☐ ☐   90   ☐

Three, four and five times tables

Activities

1. Complete the multiplication grid.

×	6	7	5	11	3	10	8
3							
4							
5							

2. Here is the price list for some sports items.

Ball	£3
Bat	£4
Net	£5

Write down how much it would cost to buy:

6 balls £ ☐   3 balls £ ☐

6 bats   £ ☐   4 nets   £ ☐

1 net   £ ☐   7 balls £ ☐

5 bats   £ ☐   12 nets £ ☐

3. Circle the correct answer for the multiplication in each box.

| 8 × 5 | 45 | 40 | 35 | 20 |

| 9 × 4 | 36 | 40 | 46 | 32 |

| 7 × 3 | 27 | 21 | 18 | 24 |

| 12 × 4 | 38 | 42 | 36 | 48 |

4. Write in the missing number to complete each multiplication.

15 = ☐ × 3   40 = ☐ × 4   35 = ☐ × 5

27 = ☐ × 3   28 = ☐ × 4   60 = ☐ × 5

9 = ☐ × 3   8 = ☐ × 4   25 = ☐ × 5

33 = ☐ × 3   16 = ☐ × 4   40 = ☐ × 5

5. This key will only open doors that have an answer that is in the three or the five times table. Colour the doors that can be opened with the key.

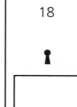

15   16   18   21

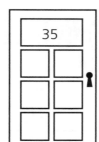

32   35   40

6. Write two different multiplication facts from the three, four or five times tables that give the answer in the circle.

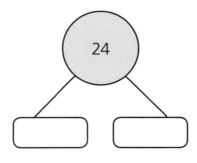

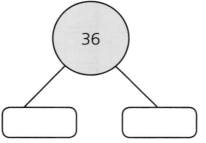

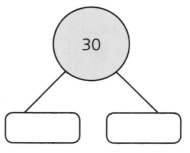

24   36   30

7. A pencil costs 3p, a pen costs 4p and a ruler costs 5p.

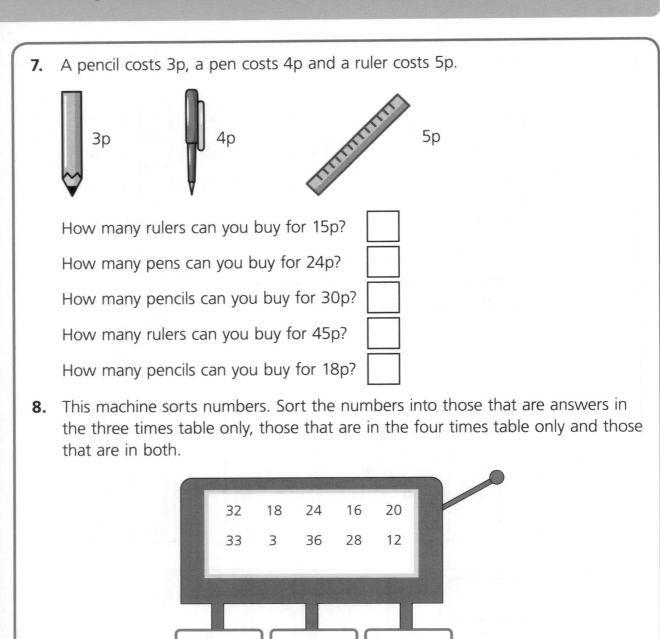

3p   4p   5p

How many rulers can you buy for 15p? ☐

How many pens can you buy for 24p? ☐

How many pencils can you buy for 30p? ☐

How many rulers can you buy for 45p? ☐

How many pencils can you buy for 18p? ☐

8. This machine sorts numbers. Sort the numbers into those that are answers in the three times table only, those that are in the four times table only and those that are in both.

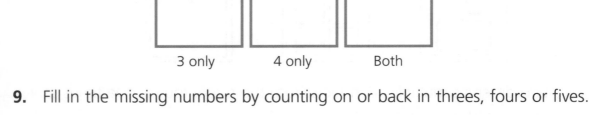

| 32 | 18 | 24 | 16 | 20 |
| 33 | 3 | 36 | 28 | 12 |

3 only   4 only   Both

9. Fill in the missing numbers by counting on or back in threes, fours or fives.

10	☐	20	☐	☐	35	☐	☐	50
16	20	☐	☐	32	☐	☐	☐	48
36	33	☐	☐	24	☐	☐	☐	☐
60	55	☐	☐	☐	☐	☐	☐	☐

10. Complete the multiplication wheels for the four and five times tables.

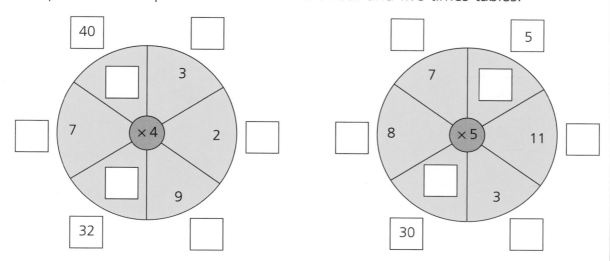

11. Circle in red the numbers that are answers in the three times table.

Circle in blue the numbers that are answers in the four times table.

Circle in green the numbers that are answers in the five times table.

1	2	3	4	5	6	7	8	9	10
11	12	13	14	15	16	17	18	19	20
21	22	23	24	25	26	27	28	29	30

Which numbers have you circled twice? ☐ ☐ ☐ ☐ ☐

12. Draw a smiley face next to the tables facts with the correct answer.

Draw a sad face next to those with the wrong answer.

5 × 4 = 20   11 × 4 = 44

9 × 3 = 24 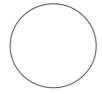   8 × 5 = 45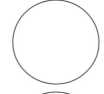

6 × 5 = 35    7 × 3 = 21

Mixed times tables

1. Work out the answer to each times table fact to complete the grid.

9 × 5	
1 × 10	
8 × 3	
7 × 4	
11 × 2	
3 × 10	

n
u
e
g
i
p

Using the code above, replace each of the numbers with the correct letters. Which animal do you make?

☐   ☐   ☐   ☐   ☐   ☐   ☐
30   24   45   28   10   22   45

2. Each arrow scores two, three, four, five or ten times the number on it. Write the score for each arrow in the box next to it.

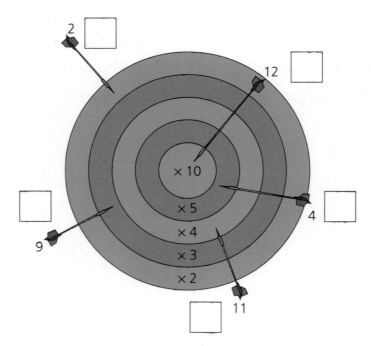

Mixed times tables

3. A calculator costs £10 and a pencil case costs £3.

How many calculators can you buy with: £20 ☐   £100 ☐   £80 ☐ ?

How many pencil cases can you buy with: £9 ☐   £18 ☐   £24 ☐ ?

4. You can work out the answers to the five times table by halving the answers in the ten times table. Write in the missing numbers to complete each pair of multiplication facts.

1 × 10 = 10	
1 × 5 = 5	

2 × 10 = ☐
2 × 5 = ☐

3 × 10 = ☐
3 × ☐ = ☐

4 × 10 = ☐
4 × ☐ = ☐

5 × 10 = ☐
5 × ☐ = ☐

6 × 10 = ☐
6 × ☐ = ☐

5. You can work out the answers in the four times table by doubling the answers in the two times table. Write in the missing numbers to complete each pair of multiplication facts.

1 × 2 = 2
1 × 4 = 4

2 × 2 = ☐
2 × 4 = ☐

3 × 2 = ☐
3 × ☐ = ☐

4 × 2 = ☐
4 × ☐ = ☐

5 × 2 = ☐
5 × ☐ = ☐

6 × 2 = ☐
6 × ☐ = ☐

6. The answers in a times table are also called **multiples**.

Here are the first five multiples of ten: 10, 20, 30, 40, 50

Write out the first five multiples of:

Two ☐ ☐ ☐ ☐ ☐

Three ☐ ☐ ☐ ☐ ☐

Four ☐ ☐ ☐ ☐ ☐

Mixed times tables

7. Circle the correct answer for the multiplication in each box.

9 × 2	18	20	22	24
1 × 4	8	6	14	4
7 × 5	30	35	40	25
3 × 4	20	16	8	12
10 × 10	110	100	120	90

8. Fill in the missing number to complete each tables fact.

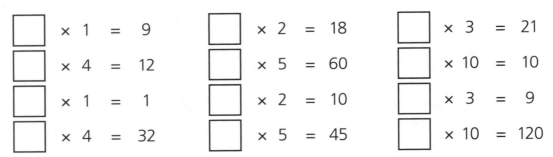

☐ × 1 = 9   ☐ × 2 = 18   ☐ × 3 = 21

☐ × 4 = 12   ☐ × 5 = 60   ☐ × 10 = 10

☐ × 1 = 1   ☐ × 2 = 10   ☐ × 3 = 9

☐ × 4 = 32   ☐ × 5 = 45   ☐ × 10 = 120

9. Colour all the shapes that contain answers in the two, three or four times tables.

What can you see? _____

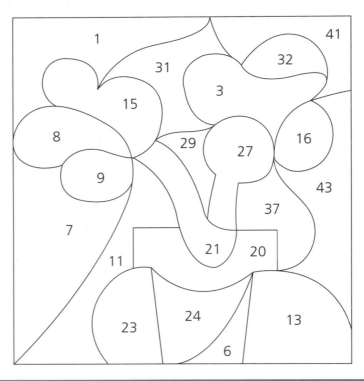

10. Complete these sets of multiplication facts.

Set 1   10 × 1 = ☐   5 × 2 = ☐   1 × 10 = ☐   2 × 5 = ☐

Set 2   3 × 10 = ☐   6 × 5 = ☐   10 × 3 = ☐

Set 3   6 × 4 = ☐   8 × 3 = ☐   12 × 2 = ☐

What do you notice? _____

11. Draw a smiley face next to the tables facts with the correct answer.

Draw a sad face next to those with the wrong answer.

1 × 10 = 10   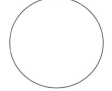   5 × 5 = 35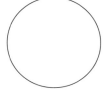

9 × 10 = 90   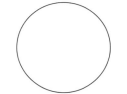   6 × 4 = 24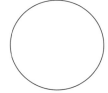

11 × 3 = 30   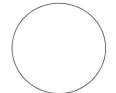   12 × 4 = 46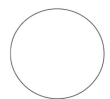

12. Shade all the multiples of three, four or five.

36	7	22	13	21
19	16	29	8	17
23	37	25	34	1
41	35	38	24	31
32	2	26	11	40

Which letter can you see? ☐

Speed test

- How many of these can you complete correctly in 2 minutes?
- Write your answers on paper. Number them 1 to 40.
- Don't worry if you cannot answer them all, just answer them as quickly as you can.
- Stop after 2 minutes, check your answers and record your score on the progress chart opposite.
- Then, try again at another time to see if you can improve your results!

Test 1

1. $4 \times 4 =$ _____
2. $6 \times 4 =$ _____
3. $9 \times 2 =$ _____
4. $11 \times 10 =$ _____
5. $6 \times 10 =$ _____
6. $12 \times 5 =$ _____
7. $10 \times 4 =$ _____
8. $5 \times 5 =$ _____
9. $2 \times 2 =$ _____
10. $7 \times 4 =$ _____
11. $7 \times 3 =$ _____
12. $3 \times 10 =$ _____
13. $8 \times 1 =$ _____
14. $5 \times 2 =$ _____
15. $4 \times 3 =$ _____
16. $9 \times 5 =$ _____
17. $2 \times 3 =$ _____
18. $3 \times 5 =$ _____
19. $10 \times 10 =$ _____
20. $7 \times 1 =$ _____

21. $1 \times 2 =$ _____
22. $5 \times 3 =$ _____
23. $2 \times 10 =$ _____
24. $3 \times 4 =$ _____
25. $10 \times 5 =$ _____
26. $3 \times 3 =$ _____
27. $1 \times 5 =$ _____
28. $9 \times 1 =$ _____
29. $10 \times 3 =$ _____
30. $2 \times 4 =$ _____
31. $3 \times 2 =$ _____
32. $11 \times 4 =$ _____
33. $6 \times 2 =$ _____
34. $5 \times 10 =$ _____
35. $11 \times 2 =$ _____
36. $6 \times 5 =$ _____
37. $4 \times 10 =$ _____
38. $6 \times 3 =$ _____
39. $8 \times 10 =$ _____
40. $2 \times 5 =$ _____

Progress chart

Colour in the stars to show your correct answers.

Attempt	1	2	3	4	5	6
Date	....	....	....	....	....	....

Scores out of 40

Attempt 1:
39 40 / 37 38 / 35 36 / 33 34 / 31 32 / 29 30 / 27 28 / 25 26 / 23 24 / 21 22 / 19 20 / 17 18 / 15 16 / 13 14 / 11 12 / 9 10 / 7 8 / 5 6 / 3 4 / 1 2

Attempt 2:
39 40 / 37 38 / 35 36 / 33 34 / 31 32 / 29 30 / 27 28 / 25 26 / 23 24 / 21 22 / 19 20 / 17 18 / 15 16 / 13 14 / 11 12 / 9 10 / 7 8 / 5 6 / 3 4 / 1 2

Attempt 3:
39 40 / 37 38 / 35 36 / 33 34 / 31 32 / 29 30 / 27 28 / 25 26 / 23 24 / 21 22 / 19 20 / 17 18 / 15 16 / 13 14 / 11 12 / 9 10 / 7 8 / 5 6 / 3 4 / 1 2

Attempt 4:
39 40 / 37 38 / 35 36 / 33 34 / 31 32 / 29 30 / 27 28 / 25 26 / 23 24 / 21 22 / 19 20 / 17 18 / 15 16 / 13 14 / 11 12 / 9 10 / 7 8 / 5 6 / 3 4 / 1 2

Attempt 5:
39 40 / 37 38 / 35 36 / 33 34 / 31 32 / 29 30 / 27 28 / 25 26 / 23 24 / 21 22 / 19 20 / 17 18 / 15 16 / 13 14 / 11 12 / 9 10 / 7 8 / 5 6 / 3 4 / 1 2

Attempt 6:
39 40 / 37 38 / 35 36 / 33 34 / 31 32 / 29 30 / 27 28 / 25 26 / 23 24 / 21 22 / 19 20 / 17 18 / 15 16 / 13 14 / 11 12 / 9 10 / 7 8 / 5 6 / 3 4 / 1 2

Speed test

- How many of these can you complete correctly in 2 minutes?
- Write your answers on paper. Number them 1 to 40.
- Don't worry if you cannot answer them all, just answer them as quickly as you can.
- Stop after 2 minutes, check your answers and record your score on the progress chart opposite.
- Then, try again at another time to see if you can improve your results!

Test 2

1. 7 × 5 = _____
2. 10 × 2 = _____
3. 8 × 4 = _____
4. 12 × 10 = _____
5. 4 × 2 = _____
6. 1 × 4 = _____
7. 8 × 5 = _____
8. 1 × 10 = _____
9. 11 × 5 = _____
10. 8 × 2 = _____
11. 9 × 10 = _____
12. 9 × 3 = _____
13. 11 × 3 = _____
14. 5 × 4 = _____
15. 12 × 2 = _____
16. 12 × 3 = _____
17. 12 × 4 = _____
18. 1 × 3 = _____
19. 4 × 5 = _____
20. 7 × 10 = _____

21. 3 × 2 = _____
22. 6 × 5 = _____
23. 9 × 4 = _____
24. 2 × 3 = _____
25. 8 × 2 = _____
26. 2 × 10 = _____
27. 7 × 4 = _____
28. 12 × 5 = _____
29. 5 × 2 = _____
30. 1 × 10 = _____
31. 1 × 4 = _____
32. 5 × 3 = _____
33. 9 × 5 = _____
34. 12 × 2 = _____
35. 4 × 4 = _____
36. 5 × 10 = _____
37. 11 × 3 = _____
38. 10 × 5 = _____
39. 10 × 3 = _____
40. 10 × 12 = _____

Colour in the stars to show your correct answers.

Attempt	1	2	3	4	5	6
Date	....	....	....	....	....	....

Scores out of 40

	1	2	3	4	5	6
	39 40	39 40	39 40	39 40	39 40	39 40
	37 38	37 38	37 38	37 38	37 38	37 38
	35 36	35 36	35 36	35 36	35 36	35 36
	33 34	33 34	33 34	33 34	33 34	33 34
	31 32	31 32	31 32	31 32	31 32	31 32
	29 30	29 30	29 30	29 30	29 30	29 30
	27 28	27 28	27 28	27 28	27 28	27 28
	25 26	25 26	25 26	25 26	25 26	25 26
	23 24	23 24	23 24	23 24	23 24	23 24
	21 22	21 22	21 22	21 22	21 22	21 22
	19 20	19 20	19 20	19 20	19 20	19 20
	17 18	17 18	17 18	17 18	17 18	17 18
	15 16	15 16	15 16	15 16	15 16	15 16
	13 14	13 14	13 14	13 14	13 14	13 14
	11 12	11 12	11 12	11 12	11 12	11 12
	9 10	9 10	9 10	9 10	9 10	9 10
	7 8	7 8	7 8	7 8	7 8	7 8
	5 6	5 6	5 6	5 6	5 6	5 6
	3 4	3 4	3 4	3 4	3 4	3 4
	1 2	1 2	1 2	1 2	1 2	1 2

Multiplication grids

Complete the multiplication grids.

Grid 1

×	1	2	3	4	5	10
1						
2						
3						
4						
5						
6						
7						
8						
9						
10						
11						
12						

Grid 2

×	2	3	4	5	10
4					
6					
11					
2					
12					
9					
5					
1					
3					
7					
10					
8					